A New Outlook

Coming out of the Grieving Place

Pastor Stephen Singleton

Edited by: Matlean Knotts

T0116859

WestBow
PRESS
A DIVISION OF THOMAS NELSON

WestBow Press books may be ordered through booksellers or by contacting:

WestBow Press
A Division of Thomas Nelson
1663 Liberty Drive
Bloomington, IN 47403
www.westbowpress.com
1-(866) 928-1240

Because of the dynamic nature of the Internet, any web addresses or links contained in this book may have changed since publication and may no longer be valid. The views expressed in this work are solely those of the author and do not necessarily reflect the views of the publisher, and the publisher hereby disclaims any responsibility for them.

Any people depicted in stock imagery provided by Thinkstock are models, and such images are being used for illustrative purposes only.

Certain stock imagery © Thinkstock.

ISBN: 978-1-4497-2877-9 (sc)
ISBN: 978-1-4497-2878-6 (hc)
ISBN: 978-1-4497-2876-2 (e)

Library of Congress Control Number: 2011918047

Printed in the United States of America

WestBow Press rev. date: 10/14/2011

To my deceased father, Nathaniel Singleton; my mother, Christine Singleton; my wife, Luciel; all my family members, especially Matt and Kayla. To the many church members and friends whose stories and witnesses came together to form the personalities in this book. And to Marie, who is the inspiration for this writing. God bless you all, today and always.

When we come to grips with our imperfections, we are more open to God's molding and remolding of our lives.

CONTENTS

PREFACE

There is no absolute method to grieving, and there is no solitary way to heal from grief. Scholars, spiritualists, and mental health professionals have offered the world several formulas to help with the understanding of our grief and the grieving process. However, I have learned through my experiences that the methods of grieving and getting beyond grief are many. The methods for grief recovery are extremely varied. What devastates one person may motivate another. Some seem to get through grief and pain in a relatively short period of time while others seemingly never get out of the grieving place. And there are a lot of possibilities in between these two extremes.

This writing is one more perspective on the subject of healing from grief. However, the lessons contained here are applicable to many aspects of healing and spiritual recovery. This book comes from over twenty years of pastoral experience and many of the people who experienced mourning and healing during those years. This writing should not necessarily replace any other on the subject. In fact, this book is more of a challenge than instruction, and hopefully it gives another perspective on the unavoidable reality that regardless of what happens to us, it is up to us to facilitate our healing. As long as we live, we will experience pain and sorrow. And when we experience pain and sorrow, it behooves us to heal or become a casualty of our anguish.

The inspiration for this book is the result of my concern for a dear friend who was overwhelmed with grief. However, the Spirit of God led me to put my thoughts on paper, and hopefully, it will help save others from being eternal victims of their pain.

INTRODUCTION

When death invades the circle of our family and friends, it can take a tremendous toll on us. It can get so bad that nothing seems normal or comfortable to us. While we are seeking normalcy in life, we may be hurting, but we can't stop the pain. We may feel helpless as we wish for the unchangeable to change. We may pray for the nightmare to cease, but we can't stop it. The pain at any given time may seem unbearable, and it seems that there is nothing that can be done about it. There is no magic formula to end sorrow. There is no secret to alter life's reality. Others may try to console us, but their words do little or nothing to ease the agony. In the meantime, the demands of life are ever-present. Family, work, school, and life's other obligations will not stop for our grief. While praying we may be tempted to shout at God: "It's not fair!" Even more tragic, we may even experience days when we want to give up.

We may feel like giving up. We may feel like surrendering to depression. We may not care if the sun rises or if life's obligations are met. While we are hurting, we may feel like crawling under the comforter and doing nothing. While we are in that grieving place, if we did nothing with the rest of our lives, we would have a ready and legitimate excuse for it. But we already know there is something in the way. We know that we do not have God's permission to give up.

God has more things for us to do. We simply can't give up on life. Furthermore, we can't give up on God, and fortunately, God has not given up on us. We have a God-given purpose in life as long as we are still alive. So let's get moving because we will not heal from grief if nothing is done about it. In the painful times of life, we may be in need of help to do what God wants us to do. We don't have to worry; God will provide that help, because God wants to help us fulfill our purpose.

Here is where we start. Before we do anything, we must honestly face our feelings. We must be candid about what we are thinking. We cannot come out of grief if we are not honest with ourselves. It does not matter what we are feeling or thinking: honesty is of the utmost importance. Moving forward will be more difficult if we are in denial about what we are feeling. We may not like what we are feeling, but we cannot get away from it.

Next, we must accept the fact that there is no justifiable reason to give up. No matter what we are feeling, we have worth. The worth we have within was given to us by God. He put it there. We will help our healing process if we recognize God's goodness in the life we are still living. Even though we may feel the burden of grief and pain, God's goodness has not been depleted, and there is always promise and potential in the time we have at our disposal. Seeking the purpose and promise in life, will help us resist the temptation to give up. The great challenge in coming out of the grieving place is in the mind. We can feel better when we make up our minds to feel better. Sometimes trying to feel better seems illogical or insensitive to the circumstances we are facing. But we should always remember that feeling better is better than feeling worse. If we don't work on feeling better, we will, without a doubt, feel worse.

The next challenge that we face is to come to some discernment about where we go from here. God never intends for us to eternally remain in the grieving places in our lives. Therefore, whether we feel like it or not, we must get moving. We won't get better until we are deliberate about moving from where we are to where we need to be.

Most important, we must candidly confront our faith in God. If we honestly feel that we can't get any better, then we are not believers in the power of God. An anchored faith in God will empower us to face anything and everything life throws at us. Life can throw some real zingers at us sometimes. However, God can empower us to handle whatever life throws at us. In fact, we gain strength when we go through life's adversity with God as our anchor. It's time to find the strength and resolve that we may have never imagined in the past. We simply need to answer one question.

DO YOU WANT TO BE HEALED?

I n the fifth chapter of the gospel of John, there is a story about an infirmed man who is lying at a pool among other infirmed and ailing people. On this particular day, a personally delivered miracle would change this man's life. He does not know it, but today is his day for decision-making. His past was most likely unfair to him, and he could not change that, but with God's help, he was about to change his future for the better.

We are often like this nameless man: unaware of the reality that any day could be our day. Every day that we are blessed to witness is a gift from God, given to us for a reason. We may be sitting among other sufferers, or all alone. We may have had a brief time with troubles, or we may have endured extended times of difficulties. Even though life may seem too unfair to press on, we will forfeit God's favor if we don't. The wisest people in the world always understand that we endure through our pain for a greater purpose. While we are enduring, God knows exactly how we are feeling, and He knows what we need.

In John chapter five, one man's appointment with healing had come. Jesus focused on the one whose time for deliverance had arrived. We don't know how God concludes these moments in our lives, but endurance will bring us to a similar juncture in our lives. This man was about to be made whole, but he could not be whole until he was asked; "Do you want to be healed?"

Jesus asked that question, because healing is fundamentally ours on the premise of a decision. Every ailing, suffering, grieving person has a decision to make. We can decide to do nothing as we fruitlessly wish to escape or change the circumstances, or we can decide that we are going to get better. I have shared this lesson with others only to be accused of being cold or indifferent to their pain. However, there is nothing cold about the question "Do you want to be healed?" That question actually acknowledges the reality of pain and shows care by inquiring about the desire to be healed.

Healing begins with a decision. In the miracle story in the fifth chapter of John, the infirmed man never answered the question because Jesus would not allow him to whine about his condition. In fact, as the man was responding with excuses, Jesus literally interrupted him and commanded him to get moving. That's the message for us today: get moving! Each day that we are paralyzed by pain is a day that we fail to grow, fail to learn, and fail to walk by faith. We can get moving in spite of pain and apprehension. If we don't get moving today, it will be more difficult tomorrow.

Jesus is teaching us in this story that He will acknowledge our condition, but He will not tolerate our excuses. He knows the chaos we experience. He knows all about the pain that is unfairly inflicted upon us. He knows how fearful we are. He understands our feelings of hopelessness. Still, He will not entertain our excuses to remain unhealed. He is teaching us that we can be healed if we want to be healed. We must answer the question before we have a chance to recover. "Do you want to be healed?

If we have decided that we want to be healed, then we may discover (or rediscover) some things that will help us get through the challenging times in life. We may not be able to see the strength that lies within, but God sees it. He can see it because He put it there. We may not know it now, but God wants to reveal it to us. If we allow the lessons and teachings of this book to become a part of life, in time, not only will we get out of the grieving place, but we will be able to help others in their trying times also.

"O Lord my God, I cried out to You and You healed me" (Psalm 30:2).

THE GRIEVING PLACE

Marie was seventeen years old when she was entrusted with primary baby-sitting duties for her older brother's daughter. This teenage girl and her infant niece, Celia, had a very special bond. Marie adored Celia, and, as the years passed, their relationship was a reflection of affection and care for each other. The whole family recognized the intimacy that existed between Marie and Celia. The family admired and celebrated this example of up-close and genuine love.

Years passed and Marie married and became a mother. Still, the bond with her niece remained intact. Celia grew to adulthood and married. Years elapsed, and Celia became a mother to three lovely children. Then the unimaginable happened. Celia collapsed at work one Tuesday morning. She was pronounced dead in the ambulance on the way to the hospital. Her death was sudden and unexpected. There were no warnings, no time in a hospital bed, no opportunities to say good-bye. Here this morning, gone this afternoon.

A young mother was gone. Three dependent children were now motherless. A young husband was alone to rear his children. A prayerful family was left stunned and shattered. As the news spread throughout the family and circle of friends, believers searched and prayed for an answer. A clan was searching for something— anything that would help ease the pain. A myriad of Bible verses said the "right things," but none of them seemed quite appropriate for the moment. When I heard about it, I called Marie.

Marie was no longer a member of my congregation because I had moved to another city. In fact, I heard about the death of her niece through mere coincidence. Marie was a beloved friend, and I wanted to express my sympathy. I had no idea what I would encounter when I called.

I made the call, unaware of the special bond she had with her niece. I expected a shocked and saddened family, but Marie was beyond shock; she was overwhelmed with grief. I thought I was calling her about her niece, but, as far as Marie was concerned, Celia was her baby before she had a baby. She used to carry Celia in her arms as her own special bundle. I don't think that I had ever encountered the kind of sorrow I heard in Marie's voice. Marie had been rendered helpless and hopeless by the tragedy.

I am grateful to God that I made the call. I am also grateful that I heard Marie clearly during that conversation. In my years as a pastor I have made many such calls to express concern and sympathy. But I wonder how many times, I may have failed to hear the person I was calling. I pray for God's forgiveness if I failed to hear an expression of pain or desperation when I made such a call. In this particular case, as Marie expressed her sorrow, I heard her torment and I literally felt her agony.

As we talked between her sobs, Marie tried to be faithful to her faith. However, she could not hide the fact that she was angry with God. The death of her beloved Celia was just wrong. Marie was in the grieving place. The grieving place is one of the worst places for the human spirit. It is the place where helplessness is the dominant sentiment, and hopelessness is the reflection of the future. We go to the grieving place when we are shocked by catastrophic developments. The grieving place is so painful that we don't just feel the pain. The pain takes over our spirit until we feel numb at best and nothing at worst. It is the place where we wind up when life has knocked us so far down, very little, if anything, matters anymore. Marie was in that place. Because she was in the grieving place, Marie was about to challenge me as I had never been challenged before. Of all the untimely deaths and unfortunate losses I had witnessed, this one seemed different.

I'm not sure why this was any different than the times I read committals over toddlers and infants. Was it more shocking than that the fire victims whose funerals I presided over? I had witnessed the sudden and shocking deaths of young adults and teens in the past. Somehow this one was singularly odd. Somehow, I knew that this episode in my walk of faith would be more significant. In this case, something more was needed to bring this to some acceptable resolve.

While we were talking, Marie kept reminding me and herself that she should not question God. Marie wanted to affirm that "God does not make mistakes," yet she felt that God had made a mistake this time. She struggled between faith and frustration without knowing that the two can occupy the same space. I was learning as I tried to console her. As I ended the conversation, I promised that I would write her a letter. I knew what I wanted to say, but I did not know how to put it all together. Several relevant lessons came to me at once. I also knew that what I needed to share with Marie is needed by practically all of us sooner or later.

"Yet regard the prayer of Your servant and his supplication, O Lord my God, and listen to the cry and the prayer which Your servant is praying before You" (I Kings 8:28).

GOD WROTE THE LETTER

I sat at the computer and I started to type: "Dear Marie." It seems that from that point, the words I wrote were not mine or under my control. The words and the message began appearing as God wrote the letter I promised to Marie. When I finished, I knew that the words were adequate and the message was clear. The two-page outpouring of the Holy Spirit was not a magic remedy or an instant fix. Instead, it was a simple message from God to Marie and all the hurting people in the world. I have learned over the years that God's message to us is always simple. Too often, we complicate what God has made simple for us. This time the message was simple and clear.

God was speaking directly to the grieving parent, the orphaned child, the widow and widower. God was speaking to the spirit broken to pieces by sudden tragedy. God was speaking to the heart torn asunder by betrayal and anger. God was speaking to everyone who has ever outlived a loved one and was left with the challenge and the obligation to carry on. God was speaking to everyone in the grieving place.

It's not easy to construct such a letter, but God specializes in things that are not easy. That's why He is God, and we are not. I was reminded that night that God is still speaking clearly to us. We can hear Him if we listen to and believe His voice. *Thank you, God, for writing that letter.*

As I proof-read the letter, I thought about the people who are among us every day who are seeking relief from grief and pain. I was reminded that we are the co-workers and classmates of people who are trying to find their way out of a fog of depression. Some of those people have stopped looking for answers to their calamities; they simply want understanding about what happens now and what happens next.

If we listen with our hearts and spirits, we will hear God speaking to us today. God is telling us not to define our existence by our disillusionments. The Bible includes examples such as David who had to continue leading and conquering after the death of two children. Job kept on praying and pressing onward after the death of his children. The God who kept David and Job will also preserve us through our sorrows. One of the specialties of God is bringing us out of the grieving place. God will help us get beyond the grieving place, if we bring our tragedy and our pain to God.

"Come unto Me, all you who labor and are heavy laden, and I will give you rest. Take my yoke upon you, and learn from Me, for I am gentle and lowly in heart, and you will find rest for your souls. For my yoke is easy and My burden is light." (Matthew 11:28–30)

BRING IT TO HIM

One of the first impulses many Christians have when tragedy strikes is to make excuses for God by blaming God. We will say things like, "God does not make mistakes," or "It's God's will." There is no comfort in those statements. It makes God appear to be some kind of sadist, entertaining Himself with our pain and sorrow. Every time I hear a believer blaming God in an attempt to console others, I cringe.

No wonder that orphan gave up on God. God took his parents. It's not surprising that the widower stopped coming to church. The preacher said it was God's will that his wife died so young. When we suffer, we need substance; the church only gave them sizzle. Poetic words and sympathy cards are not enough. When people are hurting, they need to know what to do. Our words mean very little if there is no instruction or direction in our chatter.

The best of us will nod in affirmation and make nice as casseroles and salads are left on our kitchen table, but when farewells are exchanged and the door closes, the tears begin to flow again. Grieving people do not need to hear empty words about God's reasoning regarding our tragedy. Grieving people need to know that God can and will help them heal as they come out of the painful places in life.

The Bible has already given us God's perspective on tragic developments. Remember the murder of Abel? God did not tell Cain, "It's My will." Yet, at the funeral services of shooting victims, we will say that God makes no mistakes. When the children of Job were exterminated, Job had no idea that it was not God's will that he suffer. Job could not see it, but we know that Satan was trying to break his spirit. In Job's epic story, we remember that Job said, "The Lord gives, and the Lord takes away." However, while we are reading those words, we often overlook the fact that God only gave in that story—He did not take Job's children, wealth, or health.

I have seen too much pain and suffering on this planet to believe that God designs the tragedies in our world. I have come to the conclusion that God does not place tragedy, calamity, misfortune, and heartbreak at our feet. We are supposed to bring our adversities and catastrophes and leave them at His feet. No one has ever helped their healing by blaming God for their pain. It may seem understandable to blame God. It may appear logical to point the finger at God, but in the cases I have witnessed, it seems to cause more anger. A more important step toward healing is to not see God as the author of pain and anguish, but to understand that God is the source of our healing. We bring the hurt and the suffering to God, and from there, God helps us to bear the burdens we are carrying.

This is not to imply that blaming God puts a burden on God. However, if God is to blame for our pain, then to whom do we go for our healing? When we attribute our pain to God's will, it would seem logical that we would receive more pain when we go to God with our sorrow. God is not the source of our pain. The enemy - Satan, is the source of our pain.

Humanity was in virtual perfection and bliss when the enemy deceived us into opening the portal of death in this world. One tragic conversation compelled humanity to take two bites that plunged us into an existence of pain, sorrow, shame, and death. That tragic sight was so ugly; God sealed the scene of the crime.

God never wanted us to hurt. When we hurt, God hurts with us. Since that day in Eden, God has been there to help us when life hurts us and when we hurt ourselves. Furthermore, God does not want us to bear the burden alone. We can't handle it. We may try to convince ourselves that we can handle our burdens; God is reminding us to let Him have it. He will carry us and our burdens until the time has come that we have gained our strength and realized there is still purpose and power in our lives.

"Trust in the LORD with all your heart, And lean not on your own understanding; in all your ways acknowledge Him, And He shall direct your paths" (Proverbs 3:5).

MISFORTUNE'S TARGET

Sometimes in ministry, I encounter people who feel as if they are isolated in their struggles and burdens. Their level of frustration increases as they witness family, friends, and co-workers going on with their lives as they try to hold theirs together. I listen as they tell me, "It's not fair!" Or they ask the question, "Why me?" It's understandable, but let's go back to the fifth chapter of John's gospel.

According to the story, the people at the pool were sick, blind, lame, and paralyzed. We are not told how many people were there, but we know that it was a bunch of them. It was a sight that was probably hard to tolerate. They were in a restricted place. They were isolated. Each one, to some degree, was suffering, hurting, and needing help. They were gathered at the pool because of their pain, and their desperation for help. They were detached from the general population of Jerusalem at the Sheep Gate. But they had one major redeeming factor; they were not alone. Likewise, if we take a look around our lives, we would see that we are not alone either.

When we are hurting, it may seem that we are alone and cut off from the rest of the world, but we never suffer alone. Like the people at that Jerusalem pool, we have the reality of communal connection with others. The people at the pool may not have comprehended that their assembly probably helped them to endure.

When we realize that we are not suffering alone, we are less likely to feel sorry for ourselves. There at the pool there were people who were crippled, ailing, impaired, and in need of help. Any one of them could look around and see that others were on the same path of suffering and struggle. When we are able to share in our suffering it helps us a great deal. It's encouraging to know that unfairness is not hurled exclusively at us. We are not misfortune's solitary target. There is pain everywhere.

The people at the pool in John chapter five had each other. There is no mention of conversation among them. There is no comment on how they passed the time. Could it be that the group at the pool had formed a community? Their connection through suffering and pain probably provided them with encouragement. Every morning they could see that another brother or sister had made it through the night. Just being there together made them a benefit to each other. They may not have realized it, but they inspired each other as they individually endured their ordeals to face another day.

It helps us to avoid isolation, especially if we are dealing with personal pain. We should attend worship services and enjoy the company of positive people. If we look around, we will see people laughing in their wheelchairs while others sing beautiful songs without the ability to see. There are grieving parents, orphans, widows, and widowers in our communities. If they can make it from day to day, we can too. We gain strength when we understand that we are not alone in our pain.

In September of 1989, Hurricane Hugo swept through the Carolinas heading north, taking lives and property, and disturbing my comfortable way of life. I will always remember the sound of the howling wind and the sight of the uprooted trees. Cars were flung in the water and boats were parked in the streets when that night was over. At the time, it appeared that our lives would never get back to normal.

In the wake of Hurricane Hugo, I suffered no loss of loved ones or possessions, but I endured three weeks without electricity and running water. At the time, I lived in a traditional townhouse among neighbors I did not know. During the days after Hurricane Hugo, all of that changed. In my storage room, I had a grill that burned propane gas. My neighbors had steaks and poultry. We combined our resources and helped each other get through that crazy time.

Every afternoon, for two weeks, we had a cookout. Six households on our block came together. On paper plates and with donated bottled water, we shared our food and stories. That time that could have been frustrating became "fun time" for us. We even drank donated kiddy juices with our meals. The disruption in our routines and the loss of electrical luxuries did not take away from our quality of life. In fact, I remember those days as some of the most enjoyable of my life. Every day, we talked, connected, and helped each other through the little difficulties. We looked forward to the afternoon cookouts that helped us to forget that our neighborhood looked like a war zone. We had lost some things, but we found each other. That's communion.

At the pool of Bethesda, they lacked a lot, but they had each other. When we have people to share our burdens with, we are more likely to be empowered to get through our difficulties. God is telling us today: *you are not alone.* We may feel that way, but if we look around, we will see that the world never runs out of room for people who are hurting. Yet pain is never stronger than the strength we gain when we are with others who are going through similar circumstances. Having the knowledge that God is with us should be enough, but witnesses in our lives are the just-in-case reminders that we are not alone.

"As I was with Moses, so will I be with you. I will not leave you nor forsake you" (Joshua 1:5).

IF WE CRY

Little Ted was eight years old when his father was killed. His dad was a United States Marine, killed in action less than two months after his deployment. This scene is not unfamiliar to us. Most have personally witnessed it before: the flag-draped casket, the accompanying GIs' crispy dress blues, the jolting gunfire of the salute and "Taps." The ceremony can make us cry, even if we did not know the deceased.

Ted was standing three feet from the grave with a straight pouty face, because he was told to be strong. At this tender age, he was instructed to be the man of the house. As a tear trailed down his cheek, his uncle sternly ordered him to stop crying. His uncle didn't know, but he was completely misguided. In his mind, he was giving his nephew support. In actuality, he was telling his nephew that he was not supposed to feel what he was already feeling.

I don't know how many times I have heard people say that we should not cry when loved ones die, but every time I have heard it, I wanted to smack the face that said it. God gave us the ability to cry for a reason. It is the release valve of our emotions. It's okay to cry. In some instances, crying is necessary. Read Luke 19 and John 11. We see Jesus weeping. Jesus did not weep on those occasions simply because the occasions were appropriate for His tears. The weeping of Jesus also shows us that the Divine has the freedom to weep, and we do too.

As I spoke to Marie that day, she kept saying that she knew believers are not supposed to cry. (*Hogwash!*) If God did not intend for us to cry, He would not have given us the capacity to cry. I have spoken with many people who understand the value of a good cry every now and then. Women tend to be more aware of the necessity of crying sometimes, but men also need to cry. It's cleansing and relieving. I certainly do not encourage crying, but I know that it is a natural part of being human and it has real purpose for our well-being.

Marie believed that believers are supposed to have an unwavering faith in God that would eliminate psychological agony. I have encountered many people who believe that crying in grief is an absence of trust in God. We should always remember: if we cry it does not mean that we do not trust God. God is still God when He witnesses our tears. In Revelation 21:4, it is God who wipes away our tears. God understands and God cares. We can rest our head in His lap and allow His gentle and comforting hands to soothe our sorrows. Then we are in the perfect place to allow His Spirit to heal our wounds.

Oh, by the way, little Ted was taught that crying was a sign of weakness. Imagine that attitude twenty years later when his wife needs a good cry. If his uncle did not completely pollute his thinking, big Ted may remember the need for a good cry when he remembers little Ted at his father's grave. But little Ted's pastor was standing at the head of the grave. The pastor folded his book in one hand, bent down, gave Ted a hug, and told him, "It's okay to cry, and crying does not mean that we are weak." Little Ted looked at the pastor and smiled. It's a moment in my pastoral ministry that I will never forget.

"Therefore, I take pleasure in infirmities, in reproaches, in needs, in persecutions, in distresses, for Christ's sake. For when I am week, then I am strong" (II Corinthians 12:10).

ALMOST FORGOTTEN

Valerie's voice was full of excitement when she called. She was surprised that after only three weeks past her mother's funeral, she actually laughed. She did not have a little chuckle. She had a robust, loud, uncontrollable outburst of snorts and crackles as she watched an episode of a reality television show. "Pastor, I can't believe it! I really laughed today!"

She had almost forgotten what free, open laughter felt like. Since the death of her mother, little amusements caused her to have feelings of guilt if she caught herself enjoying a moment. She had reasoned in her mind that somehow enjoying life was disrespectful to the memory of her mother. Actually, enjoying life was a great tribute to her memory. I have never heard of a deathbed promise where the dying asked the family and friends not to laugh again. I am fairly certain that deceased parents still want their children to be happy.

That happiness in available to us, because, whether we know it or not, we still have an inner desire to enjoy our lives. I gleaned that truth from many of my experiences. Those outbursts of laughter or our propensity to be drawn to entertainment are the natural tendencies for us to seek pleasure. We can't help it. God made us that way. Anyone who has no desire for pleasure or enjoyment is in serious need of professional mental help.

In the case of Valerie, she had not learned that when we are grieving, we can still laugh. It's logical. If we have God's permission to cry, we also have

God's permission to laugh. Valerie had also noticed that a few days had passed and she did not cry. I had to remind her, if she is not crying, it does not mean that she did not love her mother. She was simply progressing in her life as she was supposed to. Certainly, no one in their right mind believes that we are obligated to remain in sorrow indefinitely. Tragedies are not supposed to imprison us. Paul taught us that we are "more than conquerors" because of Christ. That teaches us that we can overcome regardless of how cumbersome life may become.

Forgotten joy, to the believer, is the hidden treasure of life. It may be concealed but it is waiting to be uncovered. We should never forget that joy is a natural part of life and an obligation for every believer. We must be cautious not to develop a self-defeating attitude when crisis comes into our lives. Examples of this are not hard to find in our world. We see it in the face of the church member who never smiles and barely speaks to others. We see it in the student who cowers in the corner of the cafeteria during lunch time and hardly says a word to another classmate. We see it in the isolated worker who is "at home" in the hidden cubicle, staring at a computer screen all day and every day, without interacting with others.

Of all the benefits we have as Christians, our right to have joy ranks near the top. When we exhibit our joy, we owe no one an explanation. When it comes to having joy, Christians do not have to pretend. We can be who we are, because God formed (and reformed) us that way. Therefore, if we cry, it is genuine. If we laugh, it is just as genuine. Too many times, we develop mental pitfalls because we are trying to live up (or down) to the expectations of others. Because we are in Christ Jesus, we know that our emotions and feelings are genuine, and it's okay to be who we are, and it's okay to feel what we feel.

Laughter is good for us, even as we live through painful situations. I have read that laughter is good for the heart, the immune system, relieving pain, relaxation, and overall mental health. Laughter is simply good for us. We are challenged to seek a reason or occasion to laugh. We can watch the situation comedies on television. We can make a phone call to that crazy relative who never seems to be down about anything. We can have a talk with that little boy or girl who loves corny jokes. Whatever it takes, we have a right to get our laugh on.

The propensity for joy never goes away. When coming out of the grieving place, we will discover that the place of cheerfulness in our lives never went away. Laughter has a way of settling the spirit as we heal. It is really life's way of reintroducing us to normalcy. That's God's way, and we should not resist it.

I once saw an artist's rendition of a laughing messiah. This rendition shows a Christ figure in a full, hearty laugh. I am usually not impressed with artistic images of Jesus, because I know that they are all imagined images. But I must admit, I like the laughing messiah. Jesus must have laughed at Peter and Thomas a few times during their interactions. I'm sure that Jesus laughed with the children of Jerusalem and Capernaum. There is something assuring in the image of a laughing Jesus. And there is assurance in the reality of our joy-filled spirit. We can laugh with certainty as we come out of the grieving place. When we find laughter during our healing time, we are assured that the night of our grief is passing and the sun is rising again.

*"Weeping may endure for a night, but joy
comes in the morning" (Psalm 30:5).*

GO AHEAD AND ASK

Maude never seemed to grieve. On the day her grandson died, it was obvious. Maude was angry at God. It's not the first time I have seen it, but it was the first time I had ever seen it with such potency. If Maude could make it to God's front door, she would have been waiting on the stoop when God came home that day.

Maude could not understand why her cute little bundle of joy had to die. Some disease she could not understand had caused his brain to swell and complications with infections were just too much for his little system to handle. His last days were spent heavily medicated, and the prayers of the family did not keep him alive.

Maude had some questions for God. At first, I tried to respond to her statements of anger and frustration. She was not asking me for an answer; she was frustrated with God. It was obvious to me that Maude did not want answers from God, she wanted an argument. I let Maude talk. I made a point to allow her to say it all. I knew it was okay for her to question God, because I knew that God can handle her questions. After a twenty-minute monologue, with tears finally forming in her eyes, she said, "We can't do anything about this, can we?"

I could only shake my head. "No."

Earlier in my career, I would have tried to stop Maude, but now I know better. No one in the Bible has ever been struck down because they questioned God. We actually get in more trouble when we stop talking to God. Just like many examples in the Bible, Maude never got a direct response from God, but Maude knew that already. It's okay for us to ask, and it is okay if God does not give us an instant response. Our faith will allow us to hold on until some resolve is finally reached.

In the letter to Marie, I wrote: "If you are frustrated, it's okay. Go ahead and punch the pillow. Scream at the ceiling if you have to." Both Maude and Marie came to realize that some of our questions are not going to be answered, and our frustrations will simply require time to subside. If we have a question for God, we can go ahead and ask. We have a right to ask; God reserves the right to answer, or not.

When parents keep information from children, it is usually because the children cannot handle it or they cannot understand it. The initial frustration of the child may seem like a response to cruelty. However, if there is enough love in the relationship, the child knows that the parent handles the things that he does not understand. We are the children; God is our Father. We trust Him when we do not understand. We cling to Him when we are afraid. In time, we realize that having Him around is assurance enough. We can be certain: God is keeping watch over us even when His voice is not heard.

Maude was angry with God, but Maude did not anger God, because Maude was honest. That's what I loved about Maude. She was mature enough to be honest with herself. We can always be honest with ourselves, and we can always be honest with God. I have experienced a strange discomfort when believers try to make others celebrate in the wake of tragedy and pain. Jesus did not throw a party when he learned of the death of John the Baptist. He went away by Himself for a while. Did He cry? We don't know. But we can be assured of one thing: in that situation, He had nothing to prove to others.

When we are coming out of the grieving place, we have nothing to prove to others. We only need to be genuine as the healing process runs its course. Whatever others bring to us, we are not obligated to pretend for them or with them. We were designed to feel, and sometimes we feel pain. There is nothing faithless about feeling pain or grief. We can be faith-filled and still be affected by life's painful realities.

I have witnessed too many final tributes marred by a cluster of pretenders. This is not to imply that we cannot celebrate the life of a departed loved one, but if the celebration does not take off, it's not necessarily because there is a lack of faith in the room. I witnessed one home-going service that started to sound as if they were glad that the deceased had died. One deacon actually said, "When I heard that Brother Hubert had died, I said, 'Praise God.'" That kind of celebration scares me. To be happy because of the departure of a loved one is unnatural. There are times when we are relieved when someone has suffered from a long illness and lost a significant portion of their quality of life. In these cases, death brings resolution to life's final transition. However, a fundamental component of being human is to feel a loss when loved ones die. It is natural to mourn when we realize that we will not see them on earth again. Human is what we are, and the feelings that go along with being human were designed by God. Actually, I think that Maude's honesty about her pain helped her get through the grieving place.

I want to share another thing about my encounter with Maude that day that I think is important. I mentioned how angry she was and how potent her anger seemed to me. But when Maude started to cry, I extended my hand to her as a gesture of comfort. Maude grabbed my hand and gently put her head to my shoulder. At that point, her sobs burst into complete release. She then firmly embraced me, and I literally felt her letting go of the emotions that were being held inside. Maude needed to physically touch someone. Maude held me for a couple of minutes as she wept in sorrow for her grandson. I felt no discomfort as I held her. I could only feel her letting go of her frustration and anger.

Everyone needs a hand to hold or a shoulder to lean on from time to time. Touching allows us to share the emotion that we are feeling. When we are expressing joy, embracing enhances the experience. When we are hurting, embracing relieves some of the load that we are carrying. For some of us, the beginning of our healing is just a hug away.

In our worship services, I often encourage our parishioners to hug each other after we have prayer. I often joke that some of us have not had a hug all day, or all week, or all month. While I joke about it, I know in my heart that sometimes it's true that some people have not embraced another human being in a long time. I know that if we go too long without a hug, we will lose aspects of tenderness and compassion. In Romans 16:16, Paul told us to "greet each other with a holy kiss." I don't necessarily recommend the kiss, but I strongly advocate the hug.

I think it is fitting that Maude was able to embrace someone as she came to grips with her questions for God. It may have seemed that God was not answering her questions, but maybe that embrace was the answer that God was offering at the moment. We may need to hug somebody when we are in the grieving place. When we hug a child of God, we are embracing God. When we embrace God, we are connecting with the most awesome force in the universe. If that's not good enough, nothing else will be.

"I waited patiently for the Lord; and He inclined unto me and heard my cry" (Psalm 40:1).

SO MUCH MORE GOING ON

Joanna was seemingly stronger than Maude. Her sister died prematurely from one of the killer diseases at the age of thirty-nine. Joanna did not shed a tear. She displayed her resiliency like a bull fighter displays his cape. Joanna was not looking for a fight with God, but it seems that she was looking for a fight with everyone else. Joanna was literally getting in the face of anyone and everyone who displayed sadness. She made sure there would be no crying over her sister.

She was waiting for the preacher when I arrived. She met me outside before I could get to the door. "Pastor, I told this family we ain't crying this week." She concluded that they spent too much time with the Lord throughout the year for them to be crying just because Bee died. Always tough, always strong, and always insisting that everyone else be that way.

Relatives and friends streamed in and out. In spite of Joanna's insistence, tears appeared and some sobbed while they shared embraces. From time to time, Joanna would give another warning about that "crying stuff." Before long, I realized that Joanna was the referee of the gathering. She was keeping an eye on everyone else; no one cared to see about her. Joanna played her role well and proved one thing to me. No one cares to see or has sympathy for the referee.

Joanna had the house in order. She took pride in knowing that people would "dry up those tears" when she came into the room. The actions of the guests started to resemble a childish game. Visitors would be talking;

35

Joanna would walk in and the room would go silent. I don't know what role Joanna thought she was playing, but it was obvious that she was a bad spirit in the house. *Bad* meaning she was the intimidator, the tormentor, and the reason no real purpose could come out of the time spent around her that day.

That was nineteen years ago. Joanna is still that way today. She is strong, loud, and avoided by practically everyone. Something tells me that there is more to Joanna than meets the eye. She shows a false sense of strength to cover up a genuine weakness. She keeps everyone else in line, and she answers to no one. In return, no one offers comfort to her. Because of her reputation, she has worked her way into social solitary. To put is plainly, no one wants to be around her.

Joanna seems to be caught in a circular current with no escape. At some point in her life, Joanna resigned herself to getting attention by being what I call the bad bully woman. Everyone knows her, and her mere presence changes the mood in a room. For her, it is unimportant that she is not liked, as long as she matters. If her presence demands attention, she matters.

It's a sad way to live. When there is no one else around to bully and keep in line, what's left? I'm sure by now she has adjusted to her role quite comfortably. It is very improbable that she will ever change. What she does not realize is that she may compel people around her to temporarily change their behavior and demeanor. Yet in the long run, she changes nothing. When Joanna set the rules that night, I realized she was sort of playing the role of God. And her role as God was poorly executed.

God allows us to go through our changes when we grieve and hurt. By allowing us to go through the phases, He enables us to change for the better. Joanna thought she was doing a good thing, but she was actually trying to get people to avoid going through the pain. We cannot heal if we do not go through the pain. We can't get through pain when we deny its existence.

God is with us as we go through the pain and through our valleys. Read the Twenty-third Psalm. Verse 4 gives us assurance as we walk *through* the valley of the shadow of death. I've been there many times. I wanted to avoid it, but I had to go through it. Still, God brought me through—every time. The Word of God never gives us assurance that we can avoid all pain; it shows us how to get through it. God's Word gives us assurance that God is with us as we get through the valleys of life. Joanna never got through her pain, so she insists that others do the same. It does not work, but that's all she knows, and no one can convince her to think differently.

I have met many people like Joanna in my pastoral ministry. I have presided over some of their funerals. In practically every case, the caring/tender spirit is missing around the house and at the home-going services. Everyone remembers that the deceased "would not want us to cry." So they don't cry. But at times, it seems as if they don't care. The people like Joanna may be very accomplished and successful, but somehow their humanness gets lost in the toughness, because being tough is all that matters to them. We can be strong and tough and still be caring and sentimental. Being strong is a good thing, but when we seem to be nothing but strong, it gives the appearance that we have no need for the compassion or care of others.

There is an unseen complexity in people like Joanna. They are direct and instant in their approach to practically everything, but that kind of existence is not practical. On the surface, there is a message of sturdiness and stability, but underneath, a lot more is going on. They can't be vulnerable, but everybody is vulnerable to something. They can't show weakness, but everyone needs help at some time or another. They can't show that they are hurting, but life is a combination of pleasure and pain. I believe that people like Joanna want to be perfect. It's an admirable goal, but it is impossible to attain. The more they push for perfection, the more imperfection rises to the surface. Furthermore, because they insist that others tough it out, they are left alone with their own pain. Over time, they help no one, and no one helps them. So they are left untouched in their imperfections.

When we come to grips with our imperfections, we are more open to God's molding and remolding of our lives. This is not to imply that we should live helplessly with a self-defeating attitude. But we should be wise enough to know that we are not perfect and we do not have to pretend to be. As far as I am concerned, pretenders are farther away from perfection than people who are honest about their pain. Beyond that, pretenders are farther away from God than they care to admit. When we don't pretend to be perfect, we are open to God's correction and God's perfecting.

The Joannas of the world need to know that it's okay if we experience sadness and pain. Grief has been around since Abraham, Isaac, and Jacob. It's still with us today, and it will be with us for the duration of time. And even as we address the stern demeanor of a Joanna, there is another tragic demeanor that needs to be addressed also. It's time for us to meet Lori.

"Therefore humble yourselves under the mighty hand of God, that He may exalt you in due time, casting all your care upon Him, for he cares for you" (I Peter 5:6–7).

THE FIGHT FOR LIFE

One Sunday after worship services, I was approached by Lindsey to accompany her on a visit to see her cousin, Lori. She described Lori as a "basket case." (The term *basket case* originally meant someone who was physically impaired to the point of needing to be carried everywhere, i.e. could be carried in a basket.) Somehow the term *basket case* evolved into a description of someone who needs serious mental help. Here is why Lindsey described Lori that way.

It had been seven months since Lori's father died. Lori was still crying every day. She was living with seven months of paralyzing grief. She needed to find her way out of the grieving place. She was as close to her father as a daughter can decently be. Lori was eleven years old when her mother died. Her father picked up the slack without skipping a beat. He was a wise father who had profound love but limited insight. Lori's father truly became both parents to Lori. He consulted female relatives when Lori made the normal transitions in her life. From puberty, adolescence, and adulthood, Lori's father was her best friend. Her father never married again, and Lori remained single also. (I don't believe that there was any incestuous behavior between Lori and her father.)

Lori was fifty-six years old when her father passed away. At first, her behavior was normal for the circumstances. Everyone expected her to grieve the passing of her father. But Lori became stuck in grief. I don't think that this was Lori's intention. It just happened. But it happened for a reason.

I listened to Lori reflect upon her father's life. She spoke admirably about his wisdom and his constant presence in her life. She could not imagine life on earth without him. Her words were divided by sobs and sniffles. It was a great testimony to the wonderful parent her father was. But Lori had a major issue to face. She had never confronted anything without her father, and now her father was gone.

Lori was an attractive woman, but sadness had taken hold of her life. Her hair was unkempt, her clothing was drab. She had a pleasant voice, but she hardly smiled. Lori had become accustomed to being in the grieving place. She was feeling at home in her sorrow. Evidence of her humanness was limited to her expression of gloom, and it was taking her life away.

Lori had to learn how to fight for her own life. If she didn't, she would have been no better off than her father, who was buried in a cemetery seven miles outside of town. I asked Lori what she wanted for her future. Of course, she wanted her father to still be there with her. That was impossible, so I pressed her for another answer. Lori was surprised by my question. She had never given that any thought. Lori was not particularly paralyzed by grief as much as she was paralyzed by the fear of facing the future without her father.

When we are stuck in the grieving place, we have to muster the courage to fight our way out. Lori had a good job, and thanks to her father, she had a very nice house. But Lori had no reference point for herself without her father. Her father meant well, but he never taught Lori how to fend for herself. Now, Lori had to accept the challenge to fight for her life or live in perpetual defeat. There was one major component of saving grace in all of this. Lori had a Christian foundation undergirding her life. This would prove to be the central component in helping Lori out of the grieving place.

Just like the man at the pool in John chapter 5, Lori had a decision to make. The question is relevant again: "Do you want to be healed?" Any answer besides a resounding yes is unacceptable. Just like the man at the pool, Lori began to make excuses when I asked the same question. "I've never faced anything like this alone." "You don't know what it's like to lose your best friend in the whole world." "I've tried, but every day I can't get back to normal." Unlike Jesus, I did not interrupt.

Finally, she asked me what she should do. I don't recommend direct advice in pastoral counseling, but there are times for exceptions, and this was one of them. After making sure that she wanted my opinion, I told her to get moving. Actually, I suggested that she move out of her house. My response was unthinkable to Lori. She was living in her father's house, and "no devil in hell" was going to get her to move. (I did not appreciate the comparison.)

Lori was right. The house belonged to her father, not her. Everything about the house was a reflection of her father. No matter where she looked, Lori could not find herself in that house. She kept running into her father's furniture, books, souvenirs, and even his clothing. Every day she lived in that house was a reminder of the life that she would never have again. Lori fought the idea courageously, for another month.

Lori revealed several things to me in the weeks after that conversation, but her persistent depression did not change. Then, on a Thursday morning, Lori called me. I saw her number on the caller ID and expected to hear her sobbing. When I answered, Lori did not acknowledge my greeting, nor was she crying. I said, "Hello," and Lori responded with, "Pastor, I owe God my thanks for the daddy He gave me."

"Yes, only God can make a father like yours." The night before, as she was praying, Lori realized that regardless of how much she loved her father, her first alliance was to God.

This was the first time Lori held a conversation with me without crying. The truth had taken root in her spirit, and now she was on the road to healing. It was strange talking with her and not hearing her sobs. I practically came to tears just thinking about the fact that she was making progress. Three months later, Lori sold the house and moved into a house that she picked out. (By the way, it was also a very lucrative move to sell the house.) Over the course of the next several months, Lori picked up her mat and walked. For the first time in her life, Lori was nest-building.

Nest-building is a time of reorganizing and reprioritizing the basic components of life. Nest-building is a good activity for our times of transition. She made decisions about decorations, furnishings, insurance, gardening, and so forth. Every so often, she would call or send a message to inquire about personal business matters or a referral for someone who could help her in her process. Lori started to thrive. Once she decided to fight through her fear of facing life alone, she blossomed into an efficient and capable woman.

Some people (like Lori) never learn how to live until they face the challenge to fight for their lives. Lori discovered herself for the first time because she moved beyond her fear of life. Lori was not unlike scores of people who get stuck in grief because they are afraid of facing the reality of living life beyond their zone of familiarity. In the case of Lori, her father had done a wonderful job of raising her, but he never pushed her out of the nest. Lori needed a nest of her own.

If Lori had never made the decision to move, it is very likely that she would have remained broken and sad, never to recover to normalcy. At first, family, friends, and neighbors would have coddled and indulged Lori's hurt with great sympathy and understanding. However, in time, Lori would have become the "strange" and isolated lady who never lived outside of her daddy's house. In the beginning, it was tragic that her father died. In the end, it would have been more tragic that she never got past his death.

Lori's love for her father was no less real when she started moving forward with her life. Somewhere between the suggestion to move and her actually putting the house up for sale, Lori realized that she had to fight for her life if she was going to do more than cry for the rest of her days. More important, Lori realized that God did not put her here to mourn her days away. I praise God for a combination of things that allowed her to gain her strength. She developed more wisdom and did not forfeit her remaining productive years on this planet. Imagine that: God is so amazing; He designed us to get better when we come through tragedy.

When I think of Lori today, I think of a tale of two women. One woman is eternally a daddy's girl. The other one discovered a new creation within herself when she refocused on her alliance to God. When Lori centered her spirit on God, it made the ultimate difference in her life. That difference is available to all of us, because God is available to all.

We cannot heal without a personal surrender (or re-surrender) to God. In Lori's situation, she did not lose her love for her loved one; she simply put things in another perspective. When Lori developed a new focus on God, she was able to develop a new outlook on her life. No matter how sweet it is to love a departed spouse, child, parent, or friend, we cannot spend the rest of our lives grieving their departure. We pay greater tribute to our loved ones when we begin the healing process and give attention to the circumstances that affect our daily well-being. When we say that we want to get beyond our grief, we are really saying that we are willing to move forward. We have unlimited opportunities to affect our future and no power whatsoever to change our past.

Another glaring lesson we get from Lori's example is this: no matter where we are in life, we have an obligation to invest more of our time, energy, and effort in our future, rather than giving our best to our past. In the case of Marie, I reminded her that her niece left three children behind who still required love and attention. Reminding her of those darling children helped her to see that there is work to be done in the future. The past is our experience; the future forever holds unlimited promise for our lives.

Allow me to share one more vital component in Lori's story. Lori was feeling abandoned by her father in the months following his death. The nerve of him: leaving her, when he had been there all of her life. She felt betrayed and let down, and she had to grow beyond that. Some of the pain in those months of crying was a lot like the pain we feel when we are betrayed in other close relationships. The fact that her father had died did not change her reliance on his presence. She felt that she needed him and would always need him. However, she later discovered that she would always need God, not her dad.

Lori took almost a year to come to grips with her feelings. Her biggest challenge was to cease the demands she made of her father and start to rely on self. When she stopped relying on her father, she could really let him go. Sounds cold? It's not. Lori had to resist the lure to take her father's death personally. Doing so only prolonged her time in the grieving place.

I remember the day Lori took me to see her new house. It was a bright, sunlit day. More than once, Lori mentioned the day's beautiful sunshine. That sunshine seemed to be a signal of God's smile on Lori that day. Lori had spent so much time indoors grieving; she lost her appreciation for the simple beauty of a sunlit day. Lori had deprived herself of that simple reminder of the light of God in her life.

Sunshine is the remnant of Eden that we still enjoy today. That same sun has been shining on humanity since our entrance into the world. Sunshine is nature's communal element for all of us to enjoy. It gives a boost to our Vitamin D; it illuminates our planet while allowing us to enjoy God's world in its entire splendor.

I often visit parishioners in hospitals, nursing homes, and residences as they heal, and I will open their curtains or blinds if the sun is shining to allow the sunlight to come into their rooms. Sunshine brightens the mood and lightens the atmosphere. Lori was enclosed in a darkened house for too long and it most likely contributed to her depression.

As Lori won the fight to reclaim her life, God put the spotlight on her. She had overcome her fear, and she was the victor that God had designed her to be. As the sun glistened on her perfectly styled hair, I realized it was God's way of showing His splendor through her joy. Thank God for courage to face what we have to face. When we win the fight for our lives, we are never the same.

"For God has not given us a spirit of fear, but of power and of love and of a sound mind" (II Timothy 1:7).

JESUS SHOWED US THE WAY

Troy was my classmate in Religion class during my freshman year in undergraduate school. Troy was the most inquisitive member of the class. That Religion class was a simple survey of the Bible, and Troy wanted an in-depth explanation for just about everything we studied in the class. Many times, his questions were probing and indicative of serious thought. He often wanted an explanation for God's logic and for the reasoning of people who followed the mandates of the Bible. By the way, Troy was an atheist. Troy was the first of a few of my classmates over the years who were atheists and studying religion. They always eliminated the chance for boredom in religion classes.

Troy's questions often made me think about what I believed, and compelled me to examine my reasoning for believing. People like Troy have always helped me clarify the path of faith that I walk. Without knowing it, Troy and others like him have assisted me with sharing my faith with other inquisitive minds. I don't necessarily miss people like Troy, but I have always needed them.

In the second semester of that year, we studied the New Testament, and Troy was even more inquisitive about the teacher we call Jesus. One day, Troy asked another one of those probing questions: "What is it about Jesus that makes Him so special to Christians?" I would have expected that question in a class on world religion. But here was Troy surrounded by more than a dozen Christian believers and he was asking a question that implied concern about the "specialness" of Jesus.

The professor paused and diverted the question to the class. Hands went up, and several answers were given. Explanations about salvation, walking by faith, hope after death, and the love of Christ were offered. Then one of my female classmates gave the answer that struck a very pleasant chord with me. "Jesus has been where we are." The answer was simple. It seemed too obvious. The answer did not make a splash in the class that day, but it made an impression on me forever.

Jesus has been where we are. This premise has been a constant foundation in many counseling sessions during my ministry. Jesus can help us because Jesus has been there and He has faced what we are facing. When we are feeling misunderstood, Jesus has been there and done that. If we are feeling isolated, we can find examples of Jesus in isolation many times over. Jesus was rejected; He experienced grief. Jesus wept in Gethsemane and on the Mount of Olives. We can be assured: Jesus has experienced every emotion we experience in our lives.

We should appreciate a Savior who has walked in our shoes and lived through the bitterness that we cannot avoid. Therefore, when we pray, we are talking to the One who knows what we are going through. He knows exactly what we are feeling. When we think that no one understands, He identifies with us. He knows the taste of salty tears. He has felt the shaking of a sobbing heart. Because of that, He cares completely and He cares absolutely. Most important, He cares appropriately. Because we know that He cares, we also know that He is perfectly able to help us.

If we are carrying the burden of grief, we also know that we don't carry it alone. "Come unto Me, all ye that labor and are heavy laden, and I will give you rest" (Matthew 11:28). What a blessing! Jesus will provide relief. That's wonderful, because we cannot carry the burden of grief by ourselves. It's too heavy, and it has a way of making everything in life seem heavier.

In my years as a pastor, I have known many people who tried to carry the burden of grief alone. They later discovered that it was too heavy. They taught me that carrying grief is not a solo endeavor. Many of them were going through the grieving process and contracted illnesses in the wake of a loved one's passing. Some may say it's coincidental, but I believe that when we mishandle or can't handle our grief, it can literally make us sick.

We must take care to be careful with the way we respond to our losses. It's shameful when we allow a bad situation to cause our lives to grow worse.

Believers can be stunned by life, but we cannot be defeated. Paul declared that we are "more than conquerors through Him who loved us." We should never forget that the love of Christ empowers us through every challenge. When we are tired, He gives us rest. When we mourn, He gives us comfort. When we are broken, He makes us over. When we die, we have already been given the power of the resurrection. That's what I call: blessed assurance.

"Therefore, since we have this ministry, as we have received mercy, we do not lose heart" (II Corinthians 4:1).

CHOICES TO MAKE

The Old Testament book of Ruth is one of my most beloved in the Bible. The story begins with a man named Elimelech and his wife, Naomi. They had two sons, Mahlon and Chilion. The family moved to the country of Moab. We are not given a timeline, but eventually Elimelech died, leaving Naomi behind with the two sons. Then Mahlon and Chilion married Moabite women: Ruth and Orpah. We are told that after ten years passed, Mahlon and Chilion died also. Three widows were left alone—without the benefit of a paternal figure in the family. Furthermore, one of those widows, Naomi, was also a grieving mother. In spite of their pain and devastation, they had choices to make—immediately. Yes, in spite of pain and devastation, challenges still faced them. (Ruth 1:9, "they lifted their voices and wept." Ruth 1:14, "they lifted their voices and wept again.") Here is another example in the Bible where people of God are weeping. Their challenge was to figure out what to do and where to go.

Times that challenge us are times for decision. While they were hurting, it was still decision time. They needed more time for healing, but decisions were still required. Most likely, they didn't feel like doing anything. Their time for grieving was overlapping their time of decision-making. Regardless of their state of mind, life was bearing down and making demands. These women understood that they had to do something. There was no time for intermission. The men were dead; the women had to move.

God does not issue us a time out when we are hurting. Seems cruel? It's not. God can see what we cannot see in ourselves. It's always the right time to move forward, whether we feel like it or not. God understands that the sooner we get moving, the sooner we move out of the grieving place. Therefore, Naomi, Ruth and Orpah had to move immediately or perish eventually.

The matriarch, Naomi, took the lead. She immediately tried to convince them to return to their homeland. At first, both of the daughters-in-law were reluctant to go back home. However, after some urging, Orpah gave Naomi a good-bye kiss and departed for home. Ruth, on the other hand, continued to resist the idea of returning home, and "clung to Naomi." Naomi tried to push her away, but Ruth broke out in poetry of timeless dimensions. Her words are found in Ruth 1:16–17:

> "Entreat me not to leave you, Or to turn back from following after you; For wherever you go, I will go; And wherever you live, I will live; Your people shall be my people, And your God, my God. Where you die, I will die, and there will I be buried. The LORD do so to me, and more also, If anything but death parts you and me."

Ruth's words were poetic, poignant, and potent, if nothing else. We are hard-pressed to find words more beautifully written or spoken. The monologue itself is the perfect wedding vow, and a verbal picture of devotion and dedication. If those words are intriguing to us in the twenty-first century, imagine what that speech did to Naomi. Ruth blew her mind.

Naomi was stunned—so much so that she was rendered speechless. The matriarch was dethroned for the day. The Scripture states that Naomi stopped speaking to Ruth. She was shocked into silence. There is no argument to counter true commitment. Absolute devotion is mesmerizing. Raw dedication can be so surprising; it dwarfs any words that may respond to it. Ruth had nothing adequate to say, so she said nothing. The two of them walked away into the sunset in peace-filled silence.

Ruth and Orpah represent two of the fundamental choices that face us when it is time to get out of the grieving place. As stated earlier, decisions are always necessary to help us get beyond the place of our grief and pain. Orpah returned to a familiar place. Ruth chose a new path for her life. There are some who would argue that Orpah's choice lacked virtue and courage, but Orpah represents those among us who find healing by returning to our roots. They reconnect with life by reconnecting with their origins. A familiar, safe, and comfortable place is the ideal place for some of us to find healing.

Furthermore, Orpah would have treasures of knowledge from her experiences to share with her people. She would not have been seen as weak or cowardly by her family members. She would have been known as one who had experiences beyond the boundaries of home. The experiences she took home would have been a blessing to them. Orpah could very well assist her own healing by becoming a resource to her people. Healing has come to maturity when we realize that we can be a benefit to others. Orpah could be a resource to grieving widows and new orphans. She had knowledge about a foreign land. She had experienced and survived real anguish. Orpah's decision does not merit criticism. She made a choice and did what she felt she had to do. Circumstances forced her to make a decision. So she made a decision and moved on. That's virtue and courage all rolled up into one Moabite woman.

On the other hand, there is Ruth, who chose to venture beyond familiar territories. Fundamentally, Ruth somehow concluded that her place in the world was somewhere beyond her home. When tragedy struck her life, she readied herself for change. If she could survive losing her husband, she could handle a foreign land. Instead of being defined by the tragedy, she decided to grow beyond it. This is another way we may help to facilitate our healing. Some people take tragedy and turn it into opportunity. There are people who "see the world" after the death of a parent or spouse. Some will pick up new hobbies or join new organizations after life hits them in the head. In either case, we can't label their decisions as right or wrong. What's right for one person may not be so for another. Some of us are like Orpah; others are like Ruth.

Another lesson from the book of Ruth is in the example of Naomi. As the story unfolds, Naomi became a widow, and she was also rendered childless. The Bible describes her bitterness, and unlike the words of Ruth, Naomi's testimony sounded almost suicidal. In between the lines, Naomi was practically affirming her worthlessness. Her fate was nothing more than a roll of the dice, until Ruth caught her off guard. Naomi did not expect Ruth to interrupt her pity party. Some of us, like Naomi, have to be caught off guard in order to realize that more possibilities await us in the future.

It is very possible that Ruth may have saved Naomi's life. Naomi's plans were vague as she talked about returning to her people. As she tried to bid them farewell, she was still mentioning how God's hand had come against her. There may have been another death in Moab if Naomi was left alone with her sorrow. But God had already sent Ruth into Naomi's life. Ruth became an agent of support and hope for Naomi. Sometimes God will send people to help rescue us when we are totally unaware of it. Ruth's loving spirit would be the conduit of God's healing for Naomi.

The book is appropriately named for Ruth, because Ruth embodies maturity, determination, and insight. Take another look at the poetic words in Ruth 1:16 and 17. Ruth is not demanding or insisting. Ruth is literally begging Naomi. "Entreat me …" The translation: "Please! Please! Please!" Ruth was insightful, if nothing else. How can Naomi say no? Ruth probably picked up her bundle and started her walk toward Judah. Naomi started a slow and laborious pace behind her, but Ruth had taken control. No more words were needed; it was time for action.

Had Ruth followed the instructions of Naomi, Naomi would have been left with nothing but burdensome thoughts about her life. Instead, Ruth became a reminder of hope for Naomi. If Ruth found Naomi worthy of that kind of love, certainly God must treasure her also. When others love us at our worst, it is a reminder of the awesome, overcoming power of God's love.

When we are in the grieving place, we should be open to the people who genuinely care about us. We are not obligated to follow all of their suggestions, but they are worthy of our attention. The love of others can and should increase our awareness of our own worth. Ruth and Naomi loved each other, and because of that, Naomi allowed herself to hear Ruth's words of devotion and concern.

The remainder of the story shows how Naomi became a mentor to Ruth. The story of Ruth would have been much different without Naomi. Is it possible that Ruth was aware that she needed Naomi? Could it be that Ruth saw something special in Naomi's life? During their better days, Naomi must have shown Ruth some admirable characteristics. As the actions and words of Ruth seem to help the saving of Naomi's life, we cannot dismiss the possibility that Ruth was trying to save her own life.

Sometimes it is necessary to save others in order to save ourselves. In this example, Ruth saved Naomi, and that would eventually assist Ruth in reaching personal greatness.

While we are in the grieving place, we should take a look around and see who may be in a position to help us. While we are doing that, we should also notice who we may be able to help. The grieving place is a selfish place. While we are there, we may lose sight of others. But practically every day we are in the presence of people who may help us, and we may also be near others who may need our help. Our worth in the lives of others does not go away when we are in the grieving place. In the case of Ruth, she could be of assistance to Naomi, or she could be in need of Naomi's assistance. It is very likely that both scenarios are true. Even today, both possibilities are available to us. We can have a positive effect on our healing if we open our hearts and look around before we do anything. We may be in the grieving place, but there are always people to help us, and there are always people around us who may need our help.

Many Bible scholars and Christian teachers teach that the book of Ruth is meant to show a vital component in the ancestry of Jesus. However, beyond that, a bundle of treasures in this story shows how the spirits of each of us are tied to the spirits of others. Regardless of circumstances or conditions, we will need others and others will need us.

"Blessed are they who mourn, for they shall be comforted" (Matthew 5:4).

WE HAVE NO CHOICE

Teddy and Janine had a good marriage. They were the fantasy couple of our graduating class. Not only were they in love with each other, they truly liked and enjoyed each other. They were just as comfortable enjoying a play as they were spending time on a blanket by the lake on a Saturday afternoon. Their relationship was an inspiration to other couples. Their love and affection for each other compelled others to love them. They were living happily ever after from the day of their wedding.

Late one Friday evening, they were involved in a head-on car collision. Teddy was injured; Janine—dead on the scene. There were speculations and questions about the accident. But ultimately, the details of the accident did not matter; a beautiful young woman was gone. Additional information was not going to change that tragedy into anything else. At the root of our healing lies the reality of accepting the painful truth.

As the news spread among our classmates, practically everyone expressed concern for Teddy. How could he go on? They were so close; so made for each other. It was one of the most unfair things we had ever known personally. We were shocked, but Teddy's example would prove to be a stellar example of healing and recovery.

Teddy had his own progression of events: funeral for Janine, physical recovery, and back to work. The normal progression of support ran its course. For the first month, hardly a day went by without someone in our circle checking on him. Three months later, maybe once a week, a friend would call or stop by. There were moments when Teddy seemed to drift into an emotional shelter as he reflected on the loss of his precious wife. To sit in his living room and hear his musings was sobering, humbling, and sad. But Teddy did not stay in the grieving place.

Six months later, Teddy was taking music lessons. He always wanted to play the keyboard, and now he was doing it. He learned to play beautiful music about life, love, and memories. He found solace in Christian music that reminded him of the constant presence of God. He still did not understand why Janine was gone. However, he knew that God would be his sustaining force as he moved forward with his life. When I asked Teddy about the self-assurance and dignity he had in moving on with his life, he replied very directly, "I had to move on; I had no choice." Morning had already arrived (Psalm 30:5).

I learned a lot from Teddy's example. I admired Teddy's emotional maturity and practical insight. It was that maturity that allowed him to choose the perfect mate for himself and also allowed him to keep his whole life in perspective. Self-improvement and self-development in milder times gave him an advantage when the hard-hitting times came along.

Teddy may be the best example I have personally encountered who faced painful realities with such composure. Teddy accepted the reality that nothing, absolutely nothing would recoup the life he had with Janine. It may be unfair, but it was real. We cannot heal until we get real with ourselves. His genuine spirit that made him a good Christian, friend and husband, was invaluable in dealing with the death of his wife.

In light of this, Teddy did not lose himself longing for a life that he would never have again. He understood that there was still more life ahead to live. Teddy moved on because he had no choice. We should not forget that life moves on with us or without us. If we don't get moving, sometimes it will leave us behind, as in the case of Lori. Other times, if we don't get moving, it will literally run us over, leaving more devastation in our lives.

The added beauty to Teddy's example is that beyond "normal" recovery, he lived beyond the moment of his deepest pain. He truly walked "through the valley of the shadow of death," and God was with him. I learned through Teddy's example that if you are a champion before tragedy strikes, you will most likely be a champion afterward. (All believers are champions, i.e. "more than conquerors.") Tragedy can change our lives, but tragedy does not have to negatively change us. Ultimately, Teddy showed us that we can make a decision to make changes for our betterment no matter what has happened to us.

Life hit Teddy with a lightning bolt, and Teddy responded with the words of Paul. *"We are hard-pressed on every side, yet not crushed; we are perplexed, but not in despair; persecuted, but not forsaken; struck down, but not destroyed"* (2 Corinthians 4:8–9). That is the perfect response to the tempests in our lives. In this passage, Paul affirmed the reality of pressure, confusion, misunderstandings, and hard knocks, but through all of it, we are secure. We can't stop the wind and rain, but we have the ultimate shelter in God's Word. We can overcome because God's Word says we can.

Teddy was able to recover because Teddy was faith-driven before Janine died. Teddy's model for life reminds us to be ready before the storm forms. Before he met Janine, Teddy was a youth leader in his church, introducing several young people to Christ. He lived the life of a Christian without shame or compromise. Because he was right with God, Teddy was prepared for what life threw at him.

Unlike Teddy, many people have to find God in the storm. They call the pastor when they get the midnight phone call, even though they only attend worship on Christmas, Mother's Day, and Easter. Some may have a slight acquaintance with the church but they want five-star treatment from the church when they are admitted to the hospital. (And the church will deliver, because that is what God's church is supposed to do.) They cry "Oh Lord!" after they have cried "Oh oh!" God will not turn them away, and the people of God shouldn't turn them away either. But, times of crisis will be a bit simpler and easier if we have developed a relationship with God and the faith community before the ominous clouds burst above our heads.

Our lives have many seasons, and it is inevitable that we will experience seasons of difficulties and hardship. Everyone knows that storm shelters are built in good weather, not after the storm begins. Teddy had a haven in Christ. When the whirlwind hit his life, he was already covered. His pain was real, but his healing was accessible, because he had a shelter in place. If we do not have a shelter, we can cry out to Christ right now. He will respond, and His response will be more than adequate.

"Therefore you also be ready, for the Son of Man is coming at an hour you do not expect" (*Matthew 24:44*).

THE FAITH FACTOR

I shared Teddy's story with a grief support group and two ladies in the room argued that because Teddy is a man, he has the capacity to get beyond trauma with greater ease and strength than a woman. I'm not sure if that's true. The story of Carl Tanzler shows that not all men are able to move beyond grief and loss. (Read *The Story of Dr. Carl Von Cosel's Obsession* by Katrina Mensies.) There is a general understanding that women are encouraged to be more in touch with their feelings. Women, are seemingly more expressive about their sentiments and emotions. However, men have the same feelings that women have. Men seem to endure more suffering in isolation. Women will run to assist a sister who is hurting; men are more likely to tell a brother, "Get over it." (Remember the uncle at little Ted's father's funeral?) Too often, men will keep feelings to themselves, because other men will not show a great deal of concern regarding their pain.

Teddy, I discovered, would really open up and talk when he knew that I was listening to what he was saying. Sometimes, when we are trying to help others who are in pain, we should resist the temptation to lead them. In many cases our effectiveness will be compromised if we do not listen. By listening, I discovered hidden strengths and virtue in Teddy that were unknown to me. As he spoke, I could recognize the power that came to life in his spirit. He needed to talk about his feelings and share his thoughts while going through the healing process.

The other thing that contributed to Teddy's remarkable progress is the fact that he was task-driven. Teddy helped his progress by finding something to do. He took music lessons. It is not unlike Lori's growth in her nest-building project. To have something to do is therapeutic, because the task helps us transition into the future. Everyone who wants to be healed should be seeking something to do. If we search, we can find something to help us move toward normalcy after tragedy and letdowns. When we are doing something, we are affirming our personal worth. Better yet, people are drawn to us when we are doing something productive with our lives. Conversely, we can be a real turn off to others when we insist on doing nothing. Teddy's life had changed because of his loss, but he created his next change by becoming his own taskmaster.

As I reflect on Teddy's example, I have come to the conclusion that Teddy's remarkable story is the result of the faith factor, not the gender factor. When people of God become faith champions, they are practically unbeatable in the arena of life. Teddy is such a man. He never had anything to prove to anyone else. (That is another reason his relationship with Janine was so special.) He was secure with God, long before that tragic accident. To this day, Teddy walks in faith, and lives by faith. Teddy proved that God is true to His promises.

Teddy's example continues to teach me as I try to teach others. When Teddy moved by faith, he showed me that we give ourselves an advantage when we approach life in faith. So if we are having a bit of trouble moving forward from tragedy, we would do ourselves good by making our first move forward in faith. Moving forward increases our chances of overcoming the damage of painful circumstances. When we move forward in faith, we seek to progress even if we do not have all the answers about our difficulties. Teddy knew that and his recovery seemed almost miraculous.

" faith is the substance of things hoped for and the evidence of things unseen." (Hebrews 11:1).

IT'S JUST OUR IMAGINATION

The Syrians were at war with Israel. While that was going on, the prophet Elisha announced the coming judgment of God and the plight of the people who would be touched by it. The prophet's voice in the Old Testament was very loud during the time of war. It's only fitting, because war changes everything. This particular war had turned former friends into foes, and the new challenges of the times were pressing the people. The trials were relentless, to say the least. War is like that. Voices shout, weapons are brandished, soldiers wield destruction; famine and destitution are rampant and people die. Meanwhile, individuals are faced with personal challenges that may be simple but certainly not easy. A good example of this is found in II Kings 7th chapter.

Four leprous Jews faced a simple but difficult decision during that war torn time. They were outside of the gate of their enemy. Their allies were absent, and they were fearful of the battle-hardened soldiers within the city. If that was not bad enough, now famine had ravaged their fields and hunger had transformed civilization into a dog eat dog arrangement. In the shadows, a menacing enemy faced them at the gate: death. They were hungry, and they had no supplies or provisions. The only thing they had was the opportunity to make a decision. Everyday life presents us with decisions. It will always be that way.

They knew that if they did nothing, they would die. If they turned themselves over to the enemy, most likely they would be executed. Their countrymen were destitute, and even if they were allowed to go to their kinsmen, they would probably be killed because of their disease. All of their options offered a greater chance for death than life. Yet, the options gave them a sense of purpose, because the options gave them something to think about and something to do.

The story affirms that life stops for no one. While these four lepers were debating what they should do, the prophet kept on proclaiming and the earth continued to turn toward another day. But there is a reprieve to this story. The enemies that the lepers feared had fled during the previous night in response to a noise sent from heaven. The lepers were worried, and yet God had intervened and their worries were unfounded. The danger was exclusively in their imagination.

Imagination is a powerful mechanism and it can cause us to think ourselves into despair. When we do not fully understand what we are facing, we tend to cower in gloom and doom. That kind of thinking is not fair to us, and beyond that, it is not fair to God. We sing praises about God's omnipotence, read scriptures about His divine characteristics, and hear sermons and lessons about His infinite wisdom. However, when we are presented with an opportunity to allow God to prove that the songs, scriptures, and sermons are true, we often talk ourselves out of trusting Him. Too often, we are vacillating without making a commitment. We are often concerned about dangers and pitfalls we cannot see. In most cases, the things we fear are only real in our imagination.

A great deal of self-destruction is due to the persuasive power of human imagination. In fact, it seems that on any given day, imagination can be more powerful than reality. When we start to imagine our demise and our defeat, it becomes easier to give up than to push on. We can literally imagine ourselves into self-defeat. The lepers in our story were on the verge of doing just that.

If imagination puts us in the place of self-defeat, only understanding will bring us out of it. Until we understand, whatever we imagine has power over our reality. When the four lepers entered the camp, they found that their fears were unfounded. Had they remained bound by their minds, they would have perished a few feet away from life-saving provisions. But it must have been grace that compelled them to try something that might work. Little did they know, God had already completed the work and all they had to do was take advantage of His favor.

We have the ability to think ourselves into paralyzing fear and depression, and we will not overcome it until we move and our thoughts are proven wrong. When we are in the grieving place, we are sometimes faced with the challenge to disagree with ourselves. It is not an easy thing to do, but we must resist the temptation of thinking ourselves into paralysis. To overcome the grieving place, we must start thinking our way out of the traps in our minds. It is very easy to talk ourselves into a corner of depression. Every question we ask ourselves can be answered with optimism, expectation, and confidence, but we often choose to answer with gloom, hopelessness, and melancholy. It takes imagination and effort to answer in the negative, and it requires the same mental resources to answer in the positive. We would help ourselves greatly by choosing to think positive thoughts.

True stories of survival and triumph tend to be about people who would not surrender when life challenged them to give up. People have survived being lost in jungles and deserts because they stubbornly clung to their purpose for living. Others have overcome horrendous persecution and devastation by giving themselves personal pep talks when reality implied that hope was all gone. Many of the great stories in history are undergirded with the stubbornness of people who talked themselves out of giving up, and we can do the same too.

I often use a sermon illustration about a man who attempted to climb a particular mountain. The mountain was rough and unfriendly to climbers. However, he was told that the mountain could be climbed in one day. Early one morning he started his climb with the intention of continuing his climb until he reached the top. He climbed all morning; then he took a short break. He then began the afternoon ascent with no plans for another break until he reached the top. He climbed until the evening fog obscured his view. After a while, exhausted, famished, and blinded by the fog, he gave up. He decided to camp for the night and start his descent the next morning. When the bright sun rays peeked over the horizon the next morning, he turned his head upward to see that there was no mountain left to climb. The fog that drifted in the previous evening was not fog but a cloud. He had made it to the top of the mountain, but the unclear view and the thoughts in his head convinced him to give up.

We could be closer to the summit than we imagined, but because of limited vision and toxic imagination we may think that we will never make it. When we are frustrated and tired, we run the risk of convincing ourselves that we cannot go on. Every day, people talk themselves into believing that there are no positives in life. That is due to the fact that they are focused on the difficulties and are ignoring the possibilities. We will never see the top of our mountain until we look upward. That's the hidden message in Psalm 121. If we are going to look to the hills, then we must look up. God will never replace all of our ups with nothing but downs. So we should keep looking up.

Both success and healing begin in the mind, not in the circumstances and conditions. When it comes to our healing and emotional well-being, it is the thought that counts the most. We cannot look upward until we think upward.

"For as he thinks in his heart, so is he ..." (Proverbs 23:7).

THE MIRACLE GOT IN THE WAY

The seventh chapter of John's gospel is the story of the sickness, death, and the raising of Lazarus. The story itself is a watershed moment in the life of Jesus' earthly ministry. It was a wonder-filled day when Jesus raised Lazarus from a four-day sleep of death. I have often wondered what we could have learned from this story if Jesus had not raised Lazarus from grave. I have given that a great deal of thought.

Think about it with me. To begin with, we have the attitudes and personalities of Jesus, Mary, and Martha. Then we have the hope-filled teaching of Jesus being the resurrection. As preachers preach about this story, they talk about the stench, the time delay, the tears of Jesus, and the grave clothes. But the miracle gets in the way of more lessons we can learn from this story.

Imagine if Jesus had arrived just as He did, with no intention of raising Lazarus. Imagine the eager approach of Martha and the quiet reservation of Mary, and Jesus simply ignoring that there is a tomb they could visit. Imagine Jesus simply paying a pastoral visit, like pastors do on a daily basis on occasions like this one. It would most likely be one of the most treasured exchanges in the Bible. I can imagine the conversation going something like this:

Martha: "Lord, if You had been here, my brother would not have died. But even now I know that whatever You ask of God, God will give you."

Jesus: "Your brother will rise again."

75

Martha: "I know that he will rise again in the resurrection at the last day."

Jesus: (Upon arriving at the house) "That is so true. Let's go and check on Mary."

Mary (Meeting them on the way): "Lord, if You had been here, my brother would not have died."

Jesus: "Martha just said that same thing. Let's sit and talk. What can I do for the two of you now that I am here?"

Mary: "I'm not sure. (Pause) What took You so long?"

Jesus: "I'm sorry that I could not be here earlier, but the journey is long and there were other matters I had to see about."

Mary: "So we were not as important as those other matters?"

Jesus: "You are always important, that is why I am here now. So let's talk."

Martha: "You know when Lazarus was sick, we did all that we could for him, but we certainly were not prepared for this."

Jesus: "It is difficult. That's because you have so much love for your brother. Yet it is even more difficult because right now you feel as if you are the only ones in the world going through it."

Martha: "That's true, because it seems that we are always helping others get through their difficulties. But it feels different now that we are going through it."

Jesus: "What is the hardest part in all of this right now?"

Martha: "Well you know you want to make all of this go away."

Jesus: "There are a lot of things we would like to make go away, but hardships are a part of life in this world."

Martha: "Since we can't make it all go away, what do you suggest we do now?"

Jesus: "That's a question you will have to answer for yourself."

Mary: "What do you mean by that?"

Jesus: "Well, the loss of Lazarus is painful, but it did not render you powerless."

Mary: "That's true, but what exactly would you recommend?"

Jesus: "Well you can think about what you can do at this time, rather than what you cannot do."

Mary: "Is that going to make us feel better?"

Jesus: "Focusing on your resources and strength will make you feel better than focusing on your limitations and weaknesses."

Martha: "You have a point there."

Jesus: "If you make an effort to do something meaningful at this place in your lives, you will always remember Lazarus's life as an inspiration for yours."

Mary: "You make it sound easy, and you know it's not."

Jesus: "I never said it was easy, but if you are going to get better, it is necessary."

Martha: "You have a way of putting things that makes you think."

Jesus: "That's good, because right now you must do more than feel; you must think."

Mary: "Wait a minute, Jesus. Lazarus was our brother and we just can't move on, just like that."

Jesus: "You sound like a man I met at a pool in Jerusalem some time back. He thought his difficulties excused him from trying to better himself. You know everything he said was true, but none of it gave valid reasoning for him to give up or feel sorry for himself."

Martha: "What if we don't feel like doing anything right now?"

Jesus: "Take your time, all the time you need. Just remember that the longer you wait, the harder it will be. We already know that pain is a part of life. There are times, like now, when we feel real pain. But in spite of all that, we can choose to stay here in self-pity, or we can choose to be believers in our own future."

Mary: "Okay, I understand. So I guess it's up to us now."

Jesus: "Yes that's about it; but guess what?"

Mary/Martha: "What?"

Jesus: "I'm going to help you through it, which is why I'm here. Truly, I am always here to help you."

That hypothetical conversation may not be the best way to show what lessons the miracle precluded that day, but it is a possible example of what we should be aware of when tragedy hits our lives. The whole process of that conversation may take days, weeks, or months, but eventually, gaining lessons from our tragedies will empower us.

A major point here is to not get stuck on things that we cannot change. If we do get stuck in that place, it will most likely lead to ongoing anger and bitterness. The other point is to not blame others who cannot change the unchangeable. When we are recovering from grief, what we have … is what we have. Some of my most frustrating times in ministry were those times when all I could do was offer a prayer and my presence with a grieving family, and a lukewarm believer thought that I should be able to do more. They were focused on the circumstances, when they needed to be focused on God and what God would have them do in the future.

Can life beat us up and down at the same time? Surely! Is it disappointing? Certainly! Is it unfair? Very unfair! Is it easy? It's not easy at all. But some things are not going to change, no matter how much we wish, pray, or complain. Getting frustrated is surrendering to the enemy. If we surrender to the enemies of grief, anger and bitterness, we will forfeit the victory that God wants us to have. Unpleasant developments may come over us, but with God's help we can become an overcomer.

"These things I have spoken to you, that in Me you may have peace. In the world you will have tribulation; but be of good cheer, I have overcome the world" (John 16:33).

WE HAVE GOD'S PERMISSION

Early in this writing, we were reminded that we do not have God's permission to give up. That truth was given to provide an eye-opening moment. That moment was supposed to be a smack in the face, i.e. a reality check. But grasping that lesson is not as easy as the teaching may sound. In the crevices of our thinking, there is a component that is always seeking and searching. Therefore, when we hear "we do not have God's permission to give up" there is a part of our spirit that is asking: "What do we have God's permission to do?" That is a great question with several possible answers.

We actually have God's permission to do an unlimited number of things. For example, God gives us permission to think about His goodness that surrounds us every day. Circumstances may cause the goodness of God to seem invisible, but we always have evidence of His goodness in the loving friends and family members who care about us. We have God's permission not to let them down, and if the love in the relationship is genuine, they will not let us down. We can find inspiration in just knowing that.

We also have God's permission to embrace our goodness and self-worth, even when circumstances may compel us not to. We have blessings that others cannot see from where they are, but we can see them where we are. We have talent, intellect, unique abilities, and a spirit that can only be shaped (and reshaped) by God and our cooperation. If we doubt that, we simply need to ask the people around us. They will gladly tell us about the good that they see in our lives. Aunts, uncles, club and church members, co-workers and our running buddies can tell us about the good we may be overlooking in ourselves. And when they tell us about the good we have within, we should believe them.

If we ever really try to count our blessings, we will quickly exhaust the day and be reminded that the blessings of God are continual and the goodness of God is immeasurable. God's goodness abides in us if we abide in Him. We have abilities, responsibilities, and opportunities that no other will ever have. There is no doubt about whether we have blessings or not. The doubt materializes when we fail to look at and appreciate our blessings.

Right now there are people in hospital beds, prison cells, and war zones who are thinking about blessings that will allow them to survive and overcome their current conditions. Likewise, there are people in penthouses and master suites who are so focused on life's shortcomings and letdowns; they can't enjoy the abundance in their lives because they do not live the abundant (spiritual) life.

Along with our blessings, we also have God's permission to do good for others in the world. When we grieve the loss of a loved one, we do not stop loving everyone else. Actually, when we provide service to others, we naturally start to feel better about living. That better feeling is the result of an understood purpose for our lives. The constant challenge in this writing has been about decision-making. Hopefully, we have decided that we want to be healed. Now, it's time to decide what we are going to do. The best choice is to do some good for others in the world.

Our presence in this world is evidence that God has a purpose for us. It does not matter how we are feeling; we are and always will be a part of God's plan and design. The plan and purpose of God in our lives always leads us to benefit others in some way. Sometimes we cannot appreciate our blessings because we may think that our blessings are exclusively for ourselves. Never! We are blessed to bless others, and until we do that, we may miss the most fulfilling aspects of being blessed.

The time of our tragedies can be the launching place to shine brighter. When we are covered with the soot from fiery trials, our bright spots are perfectly positioned to be seen by others. There in the rubble, we can find strength, resolve, resources, and faith that we were unaware that we had.

Some of the greatest advocates in the world stepped into higher purpose after horrific tragedies hit their lives.

In 1986, college basketball star Len Bias died as a result of drug use. Four years later, Len Bias's brother Jay was killed in a drive-by shooting. Their mother, Dr. Lonise Bias*, had ample reason to give up and waste away in bitterness for the rest of her life, but she didn't. Today, Dr. Lonise Bias is a motivational speaker, author, and life coach who spreads a message of hope and redemption. She reflects upon the real tragedies in her life as definitive learning experiences. Were those tragedies painful? Of course! Does she wish she could reverse those events? Sure, but she can't. She cannot change the unchangeable, but she can offer change to others. That has become her purpose, which has given substance to the senseless losses she suffered in her life.

John Walsh, who was the host of the television show *America's Most Wanted,* became an advocate for justice after the then unsolved murder of his son, Adam, in 1981. John Walsh used every bit of negative energy from that tragedy and transformed it into a positive force that helped to bring criminals to justice and closure to hundreds of families whose lives were traumatized by those criminals. He accepted the reality of an irreversible and eternally painful chapter in his life. He has, however, reversed the path for others by becoming a voice and advocate for law-abiding citizens. Because of Walsh's efforts, many wounds have been healed and many sorrows have been soothed.

In the cases of Bias and Walsh, injustice and injury dropped on their heads out of nowhere, and they responded with a will to overcome the pain instead of being overcome by it. Furthermore, they could have responded to those tragic developments with more negative energy, but they had the maturity and insight to respond with goodness. Do not be overcome by evil, but overcome evil with good (Romans 12:12). That is the godly response to the inequities of life.

So what can we do with our tomorrows? We can volunteer our time, or join (or lead) a movement, or start a service or ministry, or write a book, or visit elderly friends and relatives, or be a mentor. That, of course, is just a partial beginning to an endless list of things we can do to help others. We do not have God's permission to give up, but we do have God's permission to do something good in the world we call home.

*(Dr. Lonise P. Bias, the founder and president of Bias Consulting LLC and the Len and Jay Bias Foundation)

THE GO-FOR-IT SPIRIT

The book of Esther reads like a suspense novel, as the characters move and the plot thickens, and finally, catastrophe is diverted. The story begins with a domestic calamity in the king's palace, and the drama continues from there. Because of the disobedience of the queen, the king decided to replace her. The king's search for a new queen introduces us to Esther, and—well, it's a story worth reading, for sure.

King Ahasuerus reigned over a great region reaching from western India to northern Africa. In the northeastern portion of Africa, there was the land of Shushan, and in that place lived a man named Mordecai. Mordecai was the legal guardian of a young maiden named Esther. Esther was an orphan. Esther was Mordecai's younger cousin.

Mordecai got the word that the king was looking for a queen. He thought it would be good for Esther to become that queen. Here is the irony: Mordecai and Esther were descendants of Jews who were living in the land of foreigners due to past wars and relocation. Mordecai displayed great insight in making the decision to offer his beautiful cousin as a candidate for queen. That decision would eventually lead to Esther's efforts in protecting the future of her people. But for the purpose of our discussion, let's not overlook this interesting development after a young girl is orphaned.

It is very likely that Mordecai was very close to Esther's parents, because he took responsibility for Esther's well-being. In spite of his grief, Mordecai understood that he had to do whatever he could to provide for Esther's health and security. After making that decision, he decided to go all out and go for the best. Life did not end for them when their loved ones died. In fact, it gave them the urgency to live a more inspired and focused existence. Mordecai knew that was not the time to give up but the time to look up. Mordecai decided to reach up and go for the best.

A territory so large, and a family so obscure, and still Mordecai concluded that every young maiden had a chance to be queen. That meant that Esther was included among the young maidens who were candidates for this rare opportunity. Mordecai was willing to take the chance. The death of his loved ones became a launching place. The obscurity of their existence was of no consequence. There is no need going if we are not going for the best.

Mordecai was not satisfied with just getting beyond the place of sorrow and tears, but he accepted the challenge to aspire for the best. Mordecai had a "go for it" spirit, and we are also encouraged to have a "go for it" spirit. Mordecai had it and he passed it on to Esther. She would later challenge conventional wisdom and patriarchal tradition to have a chance to save her people. As long as we are going for it, we should go for the best. Generations into the future, John Walsh and Lonise Bias would have it. We can have that too.

Life is like an unending cycle. It will go against us for a time. After a while it flows in our favor again. When we are trying to heal, unimaginable greatness may be closer than we realize. We should go for it! Coming out of tragedy and grief can be a stimulus to toss reluctance aside and attack life with vigor. The death of loved ones often reminds us of our mortality. Unfair as it may seem, this existence will one day come to an end. So, when we look at it from that perspective, we can go for little or nothing, or we can go for all and the best. Either way, there is an expiration date in our future. It would be a great tragedy to reach our expiration date with our life's best efforts left untried. Our potential is always a mystery; our effort is always measurable.

We are being challenged right now to use that painful experience as a starting place to shoot for the highest star and reach for the best that this life has to offer. That challenge, by the way, is coming from God. Why else would He give us His son, Jesus? When He gave us Jesus, He gave us His best. When He gave us Jesus, He gave us His all. When God redeemed us, He had a "go for it" method that left nothing for questioning. Why would we offer Him anything less than our best effort? God is saying, "Go for it!" Mordecai did, and God produced a queen. God is saying, "Go for it!" Esther did and gave us a marvelous epic story of God's triumph. Imagine what God will do for us if we offered Him a "go for it" effort.

"Whatever your hand finds to do, do it with might for there is no work or device or knowledge or wisdom in the grave where you are going" (Ecclesiastes 9:10).

GOD WANTS US TO BE HAPPY

Yvette asked me to meet with her to talk about referrals for her business. Five minutes into our conversation, we were talking about her battle with stress and depression. She was a milder version of Marie, but certainly feeling unworthy of happiness. Some of her business deals had gone sour. She was raising two children on her own after a divorce. She felt misunderstood by her family and unappreciated by her friends. Ultimately, she was just tired of trying and running into what she thought were constant letdowns.

I watched in total awe as she rummaged through her purse for tissue to dab her tears. I was in awe because from my perspective, Yvette had it going on. Yvette had earned two post-graduate degrees. She was skilled at managing her money and had done well with investments. She was articulate, professional, and insightful; still she was burdened by depression. Yvette is one of many overachievers I have met who have gone through periods of depression. People who do great things with their lives tend to carry great burdens also.

Yvette recited a list of unfair developments in her life, and some of them were truly cumbersome. However, she had neglected to embrace her blessings and therefore, she could not engage in her own healing. I would point out a good I perceived in her, and she would respond with a reason not to be pleased about it.

Much like my conversation with Marie, I felt helpless as I tried to get my opinions through to her. She was not hearing me. She had convinced herself that she was justified in being bitter and sorrowful. We went back and forth for the better part of an hour and then the words fell out of my mouth. *"You have God's permission to be happy."* (Thank you, Holy Spirit!)

She stared directly into my eyes. I knew that she heard me loud and clear. There were no more tears for the rest of our conversation. She seemed to understand that it was okay to be happy. Hearing those words made a difference. In my opinion, Yvette's internal battle was not the result of the unfair developments in her life. (Everyone has unfairness to deal with.) Yvette needed a new perspective about herself. The very things that would have allowed her to enjoy the blessings in her life were the things she denied herself. In spite of her accomplishments and her intellect, she had limited vision about her future and her self-worth. Yvette needed to stop looking back and be resolute about looking forward. The gloom we experience in the present is often the result of our refusal to stop looking back.

Since that day, Yvette has not talked to me about her pain. I only pray that she has adopted that posture for her entire life. That goes for all of us. God wants us to be happy, and we have His permission to be happy. When I use the word *happy* here, I am not referring to a carnival-style giggly existence that makes us act like children who never grew up. In fact, that kind of existence is a different kind of disaster.

Actually, God wants us to have a secure emotional existence that encourages us to seek goodness in all things. God wants us to seek the good in others and in ourselves. This kind of attitude would not allow us to ignore tragedy and disappointments, but would compel us not to overlook goodness, kindness, and love. Yvette's life had burdens, but it had so much more. She was refusing to look for more. She was experiencing grief and pain because she chose to remain focused on circumstances she could not change or control.

Extended grief and pain that we experience are often because of circumstances beyond our control. We can choose to remain fixed on the enemies to our spirit or we can make the decision to nurture goodness from within. If we are weighed down with grief, depression, and emotional pain, we are probably feeding them from within. This is not to imply that these are easy to overcome. In fact, when grief, pain, and depression take root in our spirit, it is extremely difficult to rid ourselves of them. In some cases, we even grow comfortable with the agony.

But similarly, if we have the capacity to nurture continual pain, we can also feed our spirit and nurture the growth of joy and hope. We can begin the journey toward healing right now if we accept God's permission to be happy. *"I come that they may have life and that they may have it more abundantly"* (John 10:10). Unlike the message that so many preachers and pastors teach, I believe that the abundant life has nothing to do with material wealth, and everything to do with eternal riches of joy, peace, love, kindness, purpose, etc. That is the true purpose of having a Savior: to give us spiritual abundance all our lives through.

"And lo, I am with you always, even to the end of the world" (Matthew 28:20).

THERE IS LIFE AFTER DEATH

In 1999, my father passed away at the age of eighty-five. The last two years of his life were spent in a continual battle with cancer. During those two years, and he was physically limited and in the last months of his life, he was incapacitated. I received the call from my mother that Sunday afternoon to let me know that he had died. I drove the 110 miles from Columbia, South Carolina, to Charleston, South Carolina, in complete silence. I did not turn the radio on, and I made the drive in a sober trance as I reflected on his life and our time together.

When I arrived at my mother's house (my former childhood home), there were about twenty family and church members there. We embraced, prayed, cried a bit, and then there was the business of planning the funeral. That Thursday morning funeral was a "shouting good time" for sure. The choir could not sing a note without people dancing in the aisle. (That's the kind of church I experienced throughout my childhood.) My mother shouted too, and she cried also. Faith and grief were comfortably occupying the same space.

My mother acknowledged the goodness of God while saying good-bye to her husband of fifty-seven years. How could she not cry? How could she not thank God? She had spent the last two years taking care of a man whose quality of life was in constant decline. In that time, all she asked of God was the strength to take proper care of him, because she did not want him to go to a nursing home. God did exactly what she asked Him to do. To this day, my mother expresses gratitude to God for answering that prayer in the affirmative. Still, her man of almost six decades was gone, and because of that, she was grieving.

There was nothing blasphemous in her grief and nothing fake in her praise. She embodied thanksgiving and reflection as I watched in admiration. I watched my as my mother showed the world that all God wants of us is our genuineness. She had nothing to prove, and no one could entice her to put on a show to impress them. I believe that my mother has since healed adequately and carried on with grace, because she understands that there is life after death. In the case of my father, "to be absent in the body is to be present with the Lord" (II Corinthians 5:8). On the other hand, my mother had seen enough to know that as painful as it may be, she could rise from this. And she did. As of this writing, she just celebrated her eighty-ninth birthday.

I came to understand one other valuable lesson in the time after my father's passing. I learned that the things we will miss about our loved ones cannot be buried in a grave or burned in a crematorium. We don't bury the dances they had at their weddings. We cannot discard their smiles at graduation. We cannot cremate someone's laugh or the little nuances of their personalities. The world will never rid itself of the things that make us who and what we are. In the beginning, remembering those things may make us sentimental, but if we embrace what God has left us with, those same memories will eventually cause us to smile.

My father was very jovial and he loved to laugh. I can still hear his high-pitched squeal of a laugh that he used to push from his diaphragm with such power. I miss him. There are days when I wish I could talk with him or sit and watch a ball game with him like we used to do. Those things are gone, but I still hear his laugh in my spirit. I often reflect on his laid-back demeanor that always seemed to calm the moment. We buried his body, but we did not bury him. The grave cannot hold the essence of the human spirit.

Since the death of my father, I have a heightened sensitivity about how we respond to the death of a loved one. Without an understanding of the grieving place and the challenge to heal, we can practically be taken to the grave with our loved ones when they die—or we can take them with us as we live. We actually provide added meaning to their lives when we decide to be healed. When we decide to be healed, we pay a greater tribute to their memory. When we give up in response to our pain, we diminish the meaning of this gift of life that only comes from God. We should never give in to grief, because all we need in response to our grief is a new outlook on life.

A NEW OUTLOOK

It was my first year out of seminary, and I was pursuing a pastoral ministry when I really began to struggle with certain aspects of my faith. I began asking questions that were similar to the ones my former classmate, Troy, used to ask. The thing that bothered me the most was the way God's plan of salvation had to come through that ugly saga of the suffering of Jesus.

I concluded that God was the Lord of this world, and therefore He could have redeemed us with a word of His mouth or a wave of His hand. Why did that drama unfold in Jerusalem during that particular week? What is so redeeming about that story that ended with our Savior, bloody and beaten, hanging from a cross? I didn't want an answer; I wanted an argument, because all of that was so unnecessary. (At least, I thought so at the time.)

I called some of my colleagues and former classmates and asked them what they thought about my questions. I really pressed them about the need for that tragedy that made the apostles flee and the women weep. Deep down, I knew that I would not abandon my faith, but I needed another answer for my curiosity. I wanted something more palatable, more tangible, and more practical. There was a missed message in that madness, and now I wanted to see it plainly.

I left that question in the back of my mind for twenty years. I preached God's Word, shepherded God's people, and embodied everything I could to galvanize my witness for the kingdom of God. That is what faith compels us to do. It presses us onward against all logic and against all doubt.

Then in 2010, I had the opportunity to travel to Israel. For ten days I traveled with one Jewish tour guide, one Islamic bus driver, and a group of sixteen Christians (seven Catholics and nine Protestants) from the United States of America. We trekked from the northern tip of Israel, where we could see across the Syrian border to the southern region at the desert fortress of Masada, overlooking the Dead Sea. I still feel chills in my body when I think about it today.

But it was during our trip to the Old City of Jerusalem that my twenty-year-old curiosity was met by the Spirit of God. We visited the places of Jesus' final week that led Him to the crucifixion. We walked the Palm Sunday path. We strolled down the lane in the temple where He chased out the money changers. We visited Caiaphas's palace where Jesus was tried, and we spent time in the very room where Jesus stayed the night before the crucifixion. We walked the Via Dolorosa, also known as the Way of Sorrows where Jesus carried the cross. We placed our hands on the rock of Calvary. I will never be the same.

As we visited those places, I thought about Jesus' sudden decline from a hero's welcome on Palm Sunday to the humiliating arrest a few days later. I could practically hear the venomous chants to have Him killed. I imagined the passion over and over during that visit. I thought continuously about the trials, the scourging, the whipping, the spitting, the thorns, and the nails. I cried frequently as I imagined my Lord in pain, agony and humiliation. Even then I was still wondering why? I knew His pain and suffering was due to our sinful ways and despicable actions. But I knew that God was showing me another lesson as I walked where Jesus walked and touched things that were there when Jesus came to redeem humanity.

As our three days in Jerusalem were winding down, we took a trip to the Garden Tomb. (There is some disagreement about which empty tomb is the actual one that Jesus occupied.) The Garden Tomb is the one that has been generally less regarded as authentic. However, for me, the Garden Tomb experience was more compelling than the place of the Holy Sepulcher, which is the more popular of the two empty tombs.

At the Garden Tomb, we are allowed to walk inside and view the spot where the body was placed. Bars divide the public from the actual place of rest, but it was only a few feet away. While standing there, a strange sensation came over me. Then it hit me. Something I had always known suddenly had a new meaning in my spirit. The path of Jesus did not lead to the crucifixion; it led to the resurrection. Therefore if the Spirit of Christ lives in us, then the spirit of the resurrection lives in us also. If the spirit of the resurrection lives in us, we can rise from anything. That was my answer.

That drama on Calvary's hill was played out to show us something special, in spite of all the ugliness. Jesus was beat up and beat down. Jesus was cursed and insulted. Jesus was whipped and mocked. Jesus was scorned and despised for no fault of His own. Jesus was crowned with thorns and washed in sinners' salvia. Jesus was tried by unworthy judges and sentenced by the frenzy of a misguided mob. He was forced to carry a cross that was too heavy for Him to bear alone. Finally, He was nailed, hands and feet, to a piece of wood and hung between two criminals in the midday sun. Insects buzzed around His head as His body thirsted and His internal organs shut down. Finally, he could control cramped muscles no longer and he hung His head in death after uttering seven of the most remembered statements in human history. He was buried and His task was done. He said so Himself.

That same lifeless body would spring to life on the third day, and all that was done to Him in two days was gone in brief instances. Five scars were left to prove the authenticity of His resurrected body. I'm glad that the same Spirit that raised Jesus from the dead is the same Spirit that lives in us. If we have the Spirit in us that raised Jesus from all of that, we too can rise from anything. We may be grief-stricken. We may consider ourselves depressed or discouraged or disheartened. We may have been beaten, insulted, or misunderstood. Life may have us feeling tired and weary. We may be at the brink of giving up, but when we look at the cross, we can see it's empty. We can see that the tomb is empty also. He is raised, and we have that resurrection power in us. It doesn't matter what we have been through.

We have what it takes to face the challenge to push through grief. Right now may be our season of mourning. Our fairy-tale weddings may have led us to marriages that ended in divorce. We may have suffered the humiliating reality of incarceration. When we were children, we may have been abused. As trusting adults, we may have been broken by betrayal. Our bodies may be enduring hardship because of sickness and disease. Our businesses or educational aspirations may have ended in failure. Out of nowhere, at any time, our lives may suffer disastrous calamities. However, Paul told us in all these things, we are more than conquerors (Romans 8:37). That's why we bear witness to an unnecessary drama of pain, shame, and death. If we don't lose heart, eventually we will experience the resurrection.

The pain, shame, and devastation that we endure seem so unnecessary, but yet tragedy and pain are practically unavoidable. Just ask the survivors of the 9/11 attacks or one of the less fortunate victims of Hurricane Katrina or one of the tsunamis. What about the victims of nuclear disasters at Chernobyl or Fukushima? Not to mention the victims of senseless murders, mysterious diseases, and freak accidents. Actually, the normal course of life will bring us to our knees as years pass us by and friends and loved ones are laid to rest. Like Jesus, we may have wounds and scars to remind us of what we have been through, but we can take pride in the fact that we have gotten through it.

All of it is so unnecessary, but purpose comes out of it during the resurrection. It is time to be raised. Now is the time to revive God's purpose in our lives. What is most encouraging is the promise of Jesus: "Behold I am with you always, even to the end of the world" (Matthew 28:20). We can rise from anything. Isn't that a new outlook on life?

A woman stands outside of the Garden Tomb in Jerusalem.

CONCLUSION

Healing from grief and pain is about accepting the challenge to heal. We have much more power over our emotional and spiritual health than we will ever have over our circumstances in the physical world. Anyone at any time can begin the emotional/spiritual healing process that is needed for them to return to normalcy and/or reach for the fulfillment of greater potential. This writing is suitable for everyone who is willing to accept the challenge to get through pain and grief. This is not a shortcut, but it is a sure-cut for anyone who answers yes to the question "Do you want to be healed?" Accepting the challenge will lead to a new outlook on self and on life and, most important, it will lead to a new outlook on God.

ABOUT THE AUTHOR

Pastor Stephen (Steve) Singleton is a native of Charleston County, in the low-country of South Carolina, from the rural community of Red Top. His home community is a working class village with about one thousand residents and seven small "spirited" churches. He attended St. Andrews Parish High School where he participated sparsely in extracurricular activities, but he was employed as a school bus driver during his junior and senior years of high school. He graduated from St. Andrews in 1979. He then attended Allen University in Columbia, South Carolina. Feeling the need for a more multi-cultural educational setting Singleton transferred to the University of South Carolina and received a bachelor's degree in 1983. At the University of South Carolina, he served as an officer in the campus organization: Student Christian Fellowship and he also pledged Alpha Phi Alpha Fraternity, Inc. When considering seminary training, he chose another part of the country and was accepted at Perkins School of Theology at Southern Methodist University in Dallas, Texas. While in seminary, he received recognitions for campus service where he served as President of a seminarian organization and received the Karis Stahal Fadley scholarship for academic and community service. In 1988, he received a Master's of Divinity from Perkins. His early years as a pastor required him to be dually employed. His work prior to full time ministry was primarily as a non-clinical counselor for two state agencies in South Carolina; South Carolina Vocational Rehabilitation and the South Carolina Commission for the Blind. He also worked as a trainer for South Carolina Department of Health and Environmental Control. His work for the state of South Carolina gave him valuable experience in public policy and management.

He has also served as an adjunct instructor at Allen University, Benedict College, and Voorhees College. Among other subjects, he taught church history, public speaking and Bible courses. He has served as a mentor to student ministers throughout his ministerial career. His writing experience has primarily been with local publications such as: *The Upwith Herald* and *Coastal Times* in Charleston, South Carolina, and he wrote for the campus newspaper at SMU: The Mustang. He is a workshop facilitator in the areas of Christian Stewardship, Black Church History, Grief Recovery and Relationship Building. He also is a motivational speaker, and enhances his presentation by telling stories about life in rural South Carolina and the many jobs he has held while following the call of God on his life. He takes great pride in twenty-three years of pastoral experience in the Methodist tradition, but officially retired from pastoral ministry in the AME Church in 2010 and is now serving as senior minister of an independent Christian congregation, Grace Heritage Ministries in Columbia, South Carolina. Pastor Singleton is currently working on projects designed to aid in healing and recovery in the areas of physical and emotional stability through spiritual development. He loves to travel and golf. However, as the years have passed, his passion for worship, teaching and preaching continues to outgrow all other yearnings in his life. He is married to Luciel (Lucy) Hilton-Singleton, and they have two adult children: Matthew and Kayla.